MEMORIES OF LEEDS

A pictorial record of the city when we travelled by tram

by Robert F. Mack

ALLANWOOD BOOKS
Park Top, Stanningley, Pudsey LS28 6BY

Illustrations
Front cover — City Square of June 1953 showing the tramway reservation between Wellington Street and Boar Lane. The clock tower and Royal Exchange Buildings are now replaced by a tower block, whilst the Midland Bank on the right is a restaurant.

Inside front cover — A pre-1914 view of Briggate. Note the Empire Theatre on the right, now the site of a shopping arcade, and the horse cabs plying for hire. The tram depicted was built as an open-topper in 1901, but was top-covered in the period 1905 – 1907. Its destination "Cardigan Arms" was in Kirkstall Road, not far from Haddon Place.
(Photographer – anon, also page 4)

Inside back cover — One of the cars participating in the procession from the city centre referred to in the introduction, passing the Central Bus Station, watched by an interested crowd.

ISBN 0 947963 00 6

Printed by
Allanwood Press Ltd., Park Top, Stanningley, Pudsey LS28 6BY

FOREWORD

To one who was closely involved with the operation of Leeds trams during the period from 1945 up to their final disappearance from the streets, the collection of photographs which has been gathered together is both a fascinating and a comprehensive one. To the many thousands of older people who used the tram for their daily journey to and from work or for pleasure purposes this album will bring back many memories. To the younger person who has heard only stories of a legendary system this will give some indication of Leeds in the period immediately after the Second World War.

Memories tend to be short and people often fail to appreciate the radical changes which have taken place in the city within a relatively short space of time. The compiler of this book has brought together in the one volume photographs which not only show the closing days of the tramway system around which the city developed but also the numerous changes which have taken place in the last forty years.

No-one has previously done this and Robert Mack is to be complimented not only on the standard of his photography and his faithful record of the tramway fleet but also on his enthusiasm in recapturing so accurately the Leeds street scenes in the 1940's and 50's.

This is a book to be read by both young and old; it is a book to be studied by the modern historian; it is a book to be digested by those concerned with present day development; it is a book to be kept and brought out from time to time for reflection or perhaps even to settle the odd argument. The author has done a splendid job in filling what was a very large gap in the modern history of a progressive city.

Arnold Stone
(Formerly Deputy General Manager,
Leeds City Transport)

August 1984

INTRODUCTION

On the afternoon of 7th November 1959, Leeds tram 181 made the last scheduled journey from Cross Gates to Kirkgate. Later that day, ten trams ran in procession to Cross Gates, Halton and Temple Newsam, and thus ended the Leeds Tramway System.

Since that time, much of the road network and general city landscape has altered dramatically. It is therefore stimulating to reflect upon what seemed to be the permanence of an age now gone, before the private car predominated, when every self-respecting town and city boasted tram tracks in its main thoroughfares.

This book attempts to recall Leeds as it was – principally around the 1950s, although several views are included taken before that decade. Whilst trams feature in all the illustrations, the emphasis is on the backgrounds which are now replaced, and it is hoped that the scenes portrayed will arouse personal memories of an era which, for good or ill, can never return.

Robert F. Mack

Open-balcony tram 94 approaches Kirkstall Police Station along Commercial Road before the first World War.

Open-balcony tram 205 stands at West Park terminus prior to 18th April 1913, when the route was extended to Lawnswood.

"Horsfield" type tram 236 entering Cookridge Street from Woodhouse Lane on a November day in 1955. Observe the absence of motor traffic at what is now a re-aligned and tremendously busy intersection.

Top left
The 1954 City Square background of Standard Buildings has now been replaced by a modern structure, and the grime of the General Post Office on the left appreciably cleaned. Note the tramway shelters and the solitary pedestrian oblivious of, and untroubled by traffic.

Bottom left
During the War, potential extensions to the Leeds Permanent Building Society's premises in Cookridge Street were held in suspense. The view shows a "Chamberlain" type tram disgorging passengers when the delayed building work was resumed, photographed in November 1955.

Bottom right
With the former Woodhouse Moor Library in the background, the buildings in this 1956 view opposite the Eldon Hotel in Woodhouse Lane were subsequently demolished for University extensions.

Northbound in a narrow Woodhouse Lane from the top of Cookridge Street, near Cankerwell Lane, the tram track runs very near the pavement edge. The site of this 1956 scene is now adjacent to the Leeds Polytechnic, and the road configuration is completely different.

Loading in Woodhouse Lane in July 1955 outside the present Broadcasting House, then the Friends Meeting House. Fenton Street is on the right, and the old Barracks appear in the background, behind the parked bus.

The Sheepscar end of Meanwood Road of the mid-50s depicts the typical industrial background of the era.

Tram 184 loads near Barrack Street, whilst 212 takes on passengers at Stock Street with a private car overtaking. 194 enters Meanwood Road from North Street at Golden Cross. It is interesting to note that the tram 184 is operating on the final day of the Meanwood route on 25th June, 1955.

Sheepscar Library in July 1956 forms the background to this busy tramway junction, with Chapeltown Road on the left and Roundhay Road on the right.

Entering North Street from Vicar Lane in 1956, the tram approaches the well-known Arthur Cook furniture warehouse on the right, passing the mock-Tudor façade of buildings at the top of New Briggate.

Passengers disembark in Headingley Lane, at Richmond Avenue, where a "tram pinch" road sign indicates that any motorist overtaking on the nearside is likely to be nudged on to the footpath. St. Michael's Church is seen in this 1956 view.

Northbound in Chapeltown Road at Barrack Street traffic lights in 1957, tram 156 has just passed the end of the well-known Tramway Street, which ran from there to Roundhay Road. One of the street-name plates is now incorporated in a working tramway museum at Crich, in Derbyshire.

"Chamberlain" type tram 7 leaves Stainbeck Lane terminal spur to travel down Harrogate Road and run off duty into Chapeltown Depot.

St. Clement's Church and all the foreground buildings at the foot of Chapeltown Road have now been replaced by the huge road complex at Sheepscar, and only the former public library building on the right remains.

Top left
An ex-London "Feltham" type tram, passes the famous, but now demolished "Prince of Wales" Hotel in Chapeltown Road, being overtaken in carefree style by a motor car typical of the period 1957.

Bottom left
North Street in 1956 was a major traffic artery, dominated by trams and buses as this scene, near Grafton Street, shows.

Bottom right
The former Chapeltown Tram Depot is now used for industrial purposes. In 1949 the open-balcony tram parked in the entrance had been refurbished during the previous year for a documentary film featuring the wool industry, "Through the Needle's Eye"

Five trams in succession portray the typical peak hour 1956 frequency in Roundhay Road, at Enfield Road. Note the profusion of "corner shops", the rows of back-to-back terrace houses, and the school warning sign on the left pavement.

It would seem that trams queue for passengers in this 1953 Briggate scene, which displays some of the bunting used for the Coronation celebrations that year.

Note also the site clearance, on right, for an extension to Woolworth's.

A built-up North Street of 1955, looking towards Sheepscar.

North Street provides a solitary passenger for this tram, about to fork right at Golden Cross on its journey to Roundhay, amidst a trio of delivery vans.

The former "Gaiety Kinema" in Roundhay Road, at its junction with Roseville Road, is now the site of the Gaiety Public House, but when this view was photographed in 1959 the cinema was already closed.

Top right
Trams passing in Roundhay Road, at Livingstone Street, near the present Thomas Danby College. All the properties have been demolished, those on the right being replaced by light industrial development.

Bottom left
The former Congregational Church in Roundhay Road has given way to a modern building, adjoining a sheltered housing complex, but the back-to-back terraced houses in the background still remain as a reminder of another era.

Bottom right
Oakwood in 1958, where the trams left the main road and ran on a fenced reservation up to Roundhay Park. The clock tower, erected in 1904, originally stood in the City Market, but was later moved to its present location.

A former London "Feltham" tram at Sheepscar, in North Street at Golden Cross, passes the now-demolished but then famous Appleyard's Garage in 1956.

In September 1952 this ex-London tram ran driverless from Roundhay Park to Oakwood Clock, where it collided with another tram which was moving away from the stop. The car portrayed then derailed and ran on to the pavement of Oakwood Parade, narrowly missing several pedestrians.

Miraculously, no fatalities resulted, but the tram was subsequently scrapped.

A "Middleton Bogie" car, originally intended for use on the Middleton route, stands at Cross Gates terminus in August 1956. The Regal Cinema opened in 1936, closed in 1964, and was demolished to make way for a supermarket.

Snow-broom 5 heads a line of works cars reflected in the pools of what was known as the "top shed", part of the Torre Road depot complex. They were awaiting the final journey to the scrapyard at Low Fields Road, by Elland Road Football Ground. Torre Road was closed as a tram depot in 1955, but is still used as a bus garage.

A 1940 view at Hunslet terminus shows "Chamberlain" tram 135 bearing the wartime white band on the dash to make it easier to see in the blackout, whilst the masked headlamp had the opposite effect!

(above) Withdrawn trams were sometimes cut down to lower saloon level and used as bus shelters. This example offered protection to intending passengers in Otley Old Road near Cookridge Water Tower in March 1957 before graffiti and haphazard advertising posters became the norm.

Bearing a collision dint on the front panel, tram 66 traverses the unlovely and much narrower Hunslet Road, lined with shops and public houses, in April 1952.

Pre-Dragonara days at the junction of Neville Street and Sovereign Street in April 1959, prior to the rebuilding of the City Station in the background. The tram track to the right ran down to Swinegate depot and the permanent way yard in Sovereign Street, whilst Peter the Tailor and adjacent premises are now no longer there.

A busy Lower Briggate of the early-50s, when steam dominated the railway scene and the appropriately-named Viaduct Inn was dispensing Tetley's ales.

The Swan Hotel, Waterloo Road in Hunslet has now been demolished, whilst the road no longer carries through traffic from Hunslet Road.

At Glasshouse Street, the politically inspired message "cut the call-up" dominates the dreary scene in 1953 Hunslet Road, where the wall provides a resting place for local workers during the lunch break.

A sequence of views of the mid-50s showing the rural aspect of the route from Parkside to Middleton, when the line provided a pleasant scenic ride through the woods.

The Middleton bogie type trams illustrated on page 21 and centre opposite operated on this route, but the "Horsfield" and "Feltham" types shown here also rendered valuable service.

The Junction Hotel at the Dewsbury Road-Moor Road Corner almost rubbed shoulders with trams rounding the bend. Such progress is now impossible, as Moor Road is bisected by an embankment supporting the M1 southbound from the city.

The background in Church Street of 1954 is now dominated by the Hunslet Shopping Centre, whilst only the tower remains of the original Hunslet Parish Church on the right. The tram is about to turn left into Balm Road and proceed to Belle Isle.

On 21st June 1960 one of the two railcars, 601, was purchased by the Middleton Railway Preservation Society, and is seen at Parkside following delivery by low-loader. It was subsequently vandalised and burnt out in 1963.

Parkside in busier days, showing a 1958 scene and a Middleton Railway diesel shunter pausing to allow right of way to a Middleton-bound tram.

A "Middleton bogie" passes along Moor Road at the point now obliterated by the embankment supporting the M1. July 1956.

Meadow Lane in May 1956 was dominated by the tower of Christ Church, blackened by many years of industrial pollution, and now demolished. Hemingway's Ales advertised on the front of the tram recalls the days when breweries existed in much larger numbers than in present times.

A tram adapted to publicise National Savings in 1955 stands at the "Woodpecker" junction now obscured by the inner ring road flyover carrying eastbound traffic.

Meadow Lane in 1951, near the junction with Hunslet Lane, shows that motorists could be impatient even in those days!

This is the area I was born into, my "early years" were here.

The Queen's Picture Theatre in Meadow Road, Holbeck, opened as a Theatre in 1898, and became a cinema in December 1924. It closed two years after this picture was taken in 1955.

The church in the background was St. Cuthberts & Ladbroke St (No 19) was there.

I've walked up this hill many a hundred times.

The Jesse Stephenson grocery shops were part of the shopping scene in 1955, showing a tram ascending Beeston Hill towards Cemetery Road.

A tramway inspector checks traffic in Elland Road on a rainy Saturday afternoon in January 1957, where two trams were using the crossover at Hoxton Mount to return to the city and collect another load of Leeds United fans. The bus is leaving Low Fields Road for the same purpose.

This part of Elland Road, with Beeston Road junction in the background, has completely disappeared since this view was photographed in 1951.

Low Fields Road is now bisected by the M621, but in 1954 ran from Elland Road to Gelderd Road, past the Leeds United ground. A single track tramway siding extended for the entire length, and was used to store trams during football matches, and also for driver training as this scene shows.

An ex-London "Feltham" passes a "Chamberlain" tram in Tong Road, at Fifteenth Avenue, in August 1955.

Remember Wellington Road gasworks? North Sea gas has now replaced the ugly gasholders with more modern equipment thus improving the previously depressing surroundings.

Wellington Bridge in 1953, before the road improvement scheme and traffic segregation at Armley Road junction.

Top left
Two ex-London trams at New Inn terminus, Tong Road, Wortley, in July 1955. Some background buildings have since been demolished.

Bottom left
Wellington Road looks a little less drab on a sunny day in July 1956, at the gas works railway crossing.

Bottom right
"Chamberlain" tram 142 leaves the stop at White Horse Inn, Wellington Road, about to pass the bottom of Armley Road.

The famous Hayes Oyster Bar dominated the Corn Exchange loop in 1953, where trams loaded for Bramley and Stanningley. This is now part of a triangular island site fringed by bus shelters, replete with discarded drink tins and food containers, particularly at week-ends.

408 was a 1928-built tram, crossing to City Square from Boar Lane in 1953. It passes the Tatler Cinema, formerly opened in 1915 as the City Cinema; later becoming The Savoy, then The Academy. It finally ended its life as The Tatler, from 1936 to 1964, serving part of this period as a News Theatre. The premises were later demolished to make way for the present Royal Exchange House. F.G. Abe and Co. next door was famous for fountain pens and writing materials, whilst the right background is now the British Home Stores.

Two scenes at Bramley Depot, recorded in 1949 and 1953 respectively, the latter being the year the Half Mile Lane tram route ceased.

The depot opened in 1905 and was converted into a bus garage in 1949, being finally closed and demolished in 1969. The buses were then housed in a new garage further down Henconner Lane.

A city-bound tram approaches Willow Road traffic lights along Kirkstall Road under the railway viaduct carrying the Leeds-Harrogate line, a long established feature of the local industrial landscape. In 1953 the cyclist was enjoying a peaceful ride, but woe betide him if he caught his front wheel in the tramlines!

Passing the Fairbairn Lawson factory in the morning rush hour of May 1952, this tram was one of seven purchased from Manchester between 1946 and 1948. It is about to enter Wellington Street at the Wellington Road junction on the left.

The lower saloon interior of "Chamberlain" tram 84, built 1926, showing the longitudinal seating provided for 26 passengers, with room for 46 upstairs where transverse seats with "tip over" back rests were provided. This car gave 40 years of service, being scrapped in 1956, over a year after this photograph was taken.